The Gardens *of*
Thomas Jefferson's
Monticello

Text by Peter J. Hatch

And our own dear Monticello,
where has nature spread so rich a mantle under the eye?
mountains, forests, rocks, rivers.
With what majesty do we there ride above the storms!
How sublime to look down into the workhouse of nature,
to see her clouds, hail, snow, rain, thunder, all fabricated
at our feet! And the glorious Sun, when rising as if
out of a distant water, just gilding the tops of
the mountains, and giving life to all nature!

– Jefferson to Maria Cosway,

Bird's-eye view of the top of Monticello mountain with the Fruit and Vegetable Gardens on the right, or southeastern, slope of the mountain. The site for Monticello was chosen by Jefferson for its intimacy with the "workhouse of nature."

Parrot tulips blooming along the winding walk on the West Lawn

Common lilac (Syringa vulgaris)

The Workhouse of Nature

Thomas Jefferson's interest in gardening arose from a wide-eyed curiosity about the natural world. He chose the site for Monticello because of its sweeping prospects of the Piedmont Virginia countryside and intimacy with the busy "workhouse of nature." The landscape was his "workhouse" and the gardens at Monticello an experimental laboratory. Jefferson approached natural history as a scientist; he was an experimenter who aspired to observe and define seemingly all the natural phenomena "fabricated at our feet" — whether the wind direction, the blooming dates of wildflowers, or the life cycle of a destructive insect. But it was through gardening that he was able to participate in the motions of this physical world — grafting peach wood or sowing cabbages with his granddaughters. It was through horticulture that his experiments bore fruit, that his landscape assumed shape and form and color, that the unending drama of the natural world began to unfold under his personal direction.

Thomas Jefferson, Young Gardener

I have often thought that if heaven had given me choice of my position and calling, it would have been on a rich spot of earth, well watered, and near a good market for the productions of the garden. No occupation is so delightful to me as the culture of the earth, and no culture comparable to that of the garden. Such a variety of subjects, some one always coming to perfection, the failure of one thing repaired by the success of another, and instead of one harvest a continued one through the year. Under a total want of demand except for our family table, I am still devoted to the garden. But though an old man, I am but a young gardener.

— **Jefferson to Charles Willson Peale, 1811**

"Edgehill" portrait of Thomas Jefferson, by Gilbert Stuart, 1805 (Courtesy of the Thomas Jefferson Memorial Foundation and the National Portrait Gallery)

Thomas Jefferson, third President of the United States, author of the Declaration of Independence, literate in seven languages, was indeed "a young gardener." When he said, "there is not a sprig of grass that shoots uninteresting to me," or when in his garden diary Jefferson noted the appearance of a prickly poppy flower in July and remarked, "this is the 4th this year," his enthusiasm reflected not so much horticultural wizardry as an almost childlike joy in the rhythms of planting, growth, and harvest. At Monticello, Jefferson cultivated over 250 vegetable varieties in his 1,000-foot-long garden terrace and 170 fruit varieties in the eight-acre fruit garden, designed romantic grottoes, garden temples, and ornamental groves, and took visitors on rambling surveys of his favorite "pet trees." When he wrote, "the greatest service which can be rendered any country is to add a useful plant to its culture," he assumed the role of an activist plantsman, a director of new and unusual introductions in his experimental horticultural theater. Thomas Jefferson was crazy about gardening.

Oval flower bed on the East Front with tulips (Tulipa sp.), *native columbine* (Aquilegia canadensis), *Virginia bluebells* (Mertensia virginica), *and wood hyacinths* (Endymion hispanicus)

The Head and the Heart

Although universally respected for the breadth of his interests and the creative complexity of his intelligence, Thomas Jefferson has always been an ambiguous figure in the mind of the American people. Some Jefferson biographers have titled chapters in their studies, "The Head and the Heart," in reference to a personal dialogue Jefferson composed in 1786 ("Dialogue between my Head and my Heart") in which the two sides of his personality argued their case. The "head" represented the cerebral Jefferson, the man of science and rationality; the "heart" portrayed the man of passion and imagination, the human Jefferson. Both the scientific and personal Jefferson are reflected in the gardens of Monticello. On the one hand we see the scientist experimenting with seventeen pea varieties in his garden laboratory or counting the number of strawberries that would fill a half-pint jar. On the other we see a father planting tulips, the "belles of the day," with his daughters and granddaughters, a gracious friend engaging in neighborhood spring pea contests, an imaginative landscape designer conjuring up elaborate grottoes and fanciful lookout towers on his "little mountain."

Horticultural Scientist

Twinleaf (Jeffersonia diphylla)

Jefferson was a zealous record keeper. He has been described as the "father of weather observers" for his Weather Memorandum Book, a detailed account of daily temperatures, rainfall, and wind direction. His Memorandum Books reveal virtually every financial transaction that he engaged in, and he wrote as many as 19,000 personal letters in his eighty-three-year lifetime. Scholars have wondered how Thomas Jefferson accomplished anything, so busy was he documenting it all. One of his most enduring legacies is his garden diary or *Garden Book*. Published in 1944 by the American Philosophical Society, the *Garden Book* is a remarkable document, 708 pages long, detailing Jefferson's perennial horticultural enthusiasms. It includes not only his personal garden diary – a "Kalendar" of plantings in his garden, short treatises on soil preparation for grape vines, and meticulous notes on how many "grey snaps" would fill a pint jar – but also excerpts from the letters he wrote and received concerning horticulture. The *Garden Book* reveals Jefferson as a garden scientist: observing and defining the qualities of thirty-eight peach varieties or twenty sorts of cabbage; comparing three adjacent rows of green, purple, and white sprouting broccolis; proclaiming the Marseilles fig "the most delicious fig I've ever seen," or that the Europeans "have no apple to compare with our Newtown Pippin."

The staggering number of both useful and ornamental plants grown at Monticello also attested to Jefferson's experimental approach. When summarizing his most important contributions to mankind, in which he included the writing of the Declaration of Independence and the founding of the University of Virginia, Jefferson also included, in the same spirit, his introduction of the olive tree and upland rice into the state of South Carolina. Monticello was a botanic garden, an experimental station of new and unusual introductions from around the world. The geographic origins of the plants grown at Monticello reflected the reach of his gardening interests: new species discovered by the Lewis and Clark expedition like the snowberry bush and flowering currant, Italian peach and grape cultivars probably first grown in the New World by Jefferson him-

*Model of plow
fitted with Jefferson's
moldboard of
least resistance*

self, and giant, twenty-four-inch cucumbers from Ohio.

Botany, agriculture, and even surveying were other essential components that formed the foundation for his interest in both horticulture and landscape design. Monticello was the center of a 5,000-acre farm, and Jefferson regarded himself first and foremost a farmer. He helped popularize progressive agricultural practices such as contour plowing and the rotation of crops. His moldboard of least resistance, Jefferson's only legitimate invention despite his reputation as a creative inventor whose Monticello household was filled with curious gadgets, won agricultural medals in Paris in 1807. An experienced draftsman and capable surveyor (the career of his father, Peter), Jefferson was repeatedly measuring the extent of his roundabout roads or composing maps and sketches of his estate. Both skills were invaluable technical aids for his ventures into landscape design.

Jefferson was also an avid amateur botanist, and his taxonomic curiosity inspired a botanical ramble through northern New York with his friend James Madison in 1791. The woodland wildflower,

Newtown Pippin apple, from the second, unpublished edition of William Coxe's "A View Toward the Cultivation of Fruit Trees" (c. 1820)

twinleaf or *Jeffersonia diphylla*, was named in Jefferson's honor by the prominent Philadelphia botanist Benjamin Smith Barton in 1792 at a meeting of the American Philosophical Society. Barton proclaimed that Jefferson's "knowledge of natural history, especially botany and zoology, was equalled by that of few persons in the United States." Named for the butterfly shape of its leaf, the rare twinleaf grows in rich coves of the Appalachian Mountains and blooms around Jefferson's April 13 birthday.

New World Gardener

Virginia bluebells (Mertensia virginica)

Jefferson championed the use of native plants at a time when there were numerous European detractors of the American natural world. Georges Louis Leclerc de Buffon, in his *Histoire Naturelle*, argued that the New World's natural productions — plants, animals, even native people — were inferior copies of Europe's. The only book Jefferson published during his lifetime, *Notes on the State of Virginia*, was partly an effort to refute Buffon and one of the chief tenets of his thesis — that the excessive humidity in the United States crippled the biological environment. When serving as Minister to France between 1785 and 1789, Jefferson grew Indian corn in his Parisian garden and imported the seeds of American trees and flowers as gifts to his European friends, living proof of the glories of the New World forest.

Even in his ornamental plantings at Monticello, Jefferson created a pleasing blend of native and exotic plants. Wild crabs and umbrella magnolias were juxtaposed with the oriental chinaberry in his Grove; the native cardinal flower and Virginia bluebell were mixed with tulips and anemones in the oval flower beds. That he would refer to the tulip poplar and white oak as the "Juno and Jupiter of our groves" reflects his admiration for the spontaneous productions of his "workhouse of nature." Presently, two original tulip poplars straddle the west front of Monticello as a testament to Jefferson's appreciation of this soaring and majestic forest queen.

American horticulture was in its infancy during Jefferson's lifetime, 1743-1826. His association with the pioneer gardeners of the United States — nurserymen, writers, plant explorers, botanists, landscape designers, progressive agriculturists, experimental viticulturists — suggests Jefferson's vital participation in the definition of New World plants, gardens, and landscapes. Frequent correspondents included three Philadelphians: William Bartram, the visionary chronicler of the natural history of our southern virgin forest; William Hamilton, a zealous plantsman and owner of the Woodlands, a showcase horticultural estate and the best known example of the new English style of landscape at the time; and Bernard McMahon, curator of the

Strawberries (Fragaria x ananassa 'White Pine') *near the Garden Pavilion in the Monticello Vegetable Garden*

Lewis and Clark expedition, nurseryman, and author of the best gardening book published in America in the first half of the nineteenth century, *The American Gardener's Calendar*, which has been described as Jefferson's horticultural "bible." Furthermore, Jefferson's sponsorship of the Lewis and Clark expedition (which was, in part, considered a botanical exploration) and his role in co-founding both the Albemarle Agricultural Society and American Philosophical Society set a lofty standard for the promotion of scientific exploration by an American public servant.

Humanized Horticulture

The gardens at Monticello were nourished generously by a society of international gardeners. For Jefferson, plants were intimately associated with people – friends, neighbors, political allies – and the exchange of seeds, bulbs, and fruit scions a token of enduring friendship. Margaret Bayard Smith, a Washington friend, wrote to Jefferson requesting a geranium plant that was growing in the windowed cabinet of the President's House (now the White House). She mentioned how the plant would be watered with her "tears of regret" at his retirement to Monticello. Jefferson responded in 1809:

Rembrandt Peale, *"Rubens Peale with a Geranium," 1801,*
Patrons' Permanent Fund, ©1992 National Gallery of Art, Washington, D.C.

It is in very bad condition, having been neglected latterly, as not intended to be removed. He [Jefferson] cannot give it his parting blessing more effectually than by consigning it to the nourishing hand of Mrs. Smith. If plants have sensibility, as the analogy of their organisation with ours seems to indicate, it cannot but be proudly sensible of her fostering attentions. Of his regrets at parting with the society of Washington, a very sensible portion attaches itself to Mrs. Smith, whose friendship he has particularly valued.

Garden peas (Pisum sativum)

This union of gardening and sociability is evident throughout the letters in the *Garden Book*. Jefferson would chide his daughters and granddaughters for their inattention to the flower beds around the house, while they in turn would report on the latest horticultural dramas taking place at Monticello: how the overseer, Edmund Bacon, had mistakenly covered the lawn with charcoal rather than manure, or that the kitchen garden, "at a distance . . . looks very green but . . . does not bear close examination, the weeds having taken possession of much the greater part of it." Ellen Randolph Coolidge, Jefferson's granddaughter, recalled the heyday of flower gardening at Monticello: "When the flowers were in bloom, and we were in ecstasies over the rich purple and crimson, or pure white, or delicate lilac, or pale yellow of the blossoms, how he would sympathize in our admiration, or discuss . . . new groupings and combinations and contrasts. Oh, these were happy moments for us and for him." The gardening process brought the Jefferson family closer together.

Jefferson also engaged in friendly competitions with his neighbors to determine who could bring the first English pea to the table in late Spring, the winner then hosting a community dinner that included a feast on the winning dish (or teaspoon) of peas. One neighbor, George Divers, proudly regarded himself as the perennial, undisputed champion of the pea contest. When, one year, Jefferson harvested the first neighborhood pea, the sage of Monticello refused to divulge his victory in fear of rocking the pride of his friend.

Wholesome Balance

Lettuce (Lactuca sativa 'Tennis-ball')

Jefferson's essential philosophy of gardening was perhaps best summarized in a letter to his daughter Martha after she complained of insect-riddled plants in the Monticello vegetable garden: "We will try this winter to cover our garden with a heavy coating of manure. When earth is rich it bids defiance to droughts, yields in abundance, and of the best quality. I suspect that the insects which have harassed you have been encouraged by the feebleness of your plants; and that has been produced by the lean state of the soil. We will attack them another year with joint efforts." Such commitment to the regenerative powers of soil improvement suggests Jefferson's belief in the wholesome balance of nature and gardening. His response to the damage inflicted by the Hessian fly on his wheat crop revealed more a naturalist's curiosity about an insect's life cycle than a farmer's quest for a successful harvest. Weeds were a source of green manure rather than a threat to his crops. When Jefferson wrote that, for a gardener, "the failure of one thing is repaired by the success of another," he was expressing further this holistic approach to horticulture.

The evolution of Thomas Jefferson's horticultural experiments paralleled the extent of his residency at Monticello; when he was away as governor of Virginia, member of Congress, minister to France, vice president, and President of the United States, attention to the gardens inevitably suffered. On the other hand, he always returned from public service with ambitious horticultural designs – plants, plans, and renewed energy to direct toward the improvement of his estate.

Gardening was a welcome retreat from the slings and arrows of political life. In 1807 Jefferson wrote Timothy Matlack, a Pennsylvania fruit grower, and asked for pears, peaches, and grapes. He added, "I shall be able to carry & plant them myself at Monticello where I shall then begin to occupy myself according to my own natural inclinations, which have been so long kept down by the history of our times." The spring of 1807 was the most ambitious and creative gardening period in Jefferson's horticultural career: the vineyards were revived with intensive plantings of twenty-four varieties of

Garden Pavilion and pole beans

European grape, and the oval flower beds were designed and planted. This was also the most painful period of Jefferson's presidency as he suffered the periodic headaches that accompanied his involvement in the contentious Aaron Burr treason trial.

Thomas Jefferson was a planter. A total of 1,031 fruit trees were set out in his South Orchard alone. He documented planting at Monticello approximately 113 species of ornamental trees and sixty-five shrubs, over 100 species of herbaceous plants in his flower gardens, and 450 varieties of ninety-five species of fruits, vegetables, nuts, and herbs. The success or failure of his horticultural experiments was inconsequential compared to the example of his stewardship. Jefferson's enthusiasm often outstripped his practical capability, and the saga of many horticultural projects, from grape culture to sugar maple plantations, began with dreamy visions that dissolved before the harsh realities of the Virginia climate and an unruly plantation structure. The history of gardening at Monticello is not so much a testament to Thomas Jefferson's horticultural triumphs as it is a reflection of the Jefferson spirit — expansive, optimistic, innocent, epicurean — very American.

Landscape Architect

Jefferson's plan for creating a ferme ornée at Monticello — the "articles of minor husbandry" were experimental field crop plots (top), while the "attributes of a garden" were represented by the spiral labyrinth of scotch broom (center) (Courtesy of The Huntington Library, San Marino, California)

In a letter to his granddaughter, Ellen, in 1805, Jefferson discussed the precise number of fine arts: "Many reckon but 5: painting, sculpture, architecture, music & poetry. To these some have added Oratory . . . . Others again add Gardening as a 7th fine art. Not horticulture, but the art of embellishing grounds by fancy." Jefferson composed numerous fanciful schemes for the landscape at Monticello. He sketched over twenty designs for ornamental garden structures, some intended for the summit of Montalto ("high mountain"), which towers over Monticello ("little mountain") to the south. He also proposed a series of cascading waterfalls for Montalto and a romantic, classical grotto for the North spring at Monticello. Most of these ambitious plans were never realized.

Jefferson toured English gardens in 1786 while serving as Minister to France. Upon his return, he wrote, "the gardening in that country is the article in which it surpasses all the earth, I mean their pleasure gardening." He was impressed by the newest landscape style in which garden designers attempted to imitate the picturesque schemes of eighteenth-century landscape painters and soften the distinctions between garden, park, and English countryside. This was a radical departure from the traditional geometric gardens of Europe.

This visit to England inspired many of Jefferson's ideas for the landscape at Monticello, including the planting of trees in clumps, the informal roundabout flower walk, and the Grove or ornamental forest. It also stimulated Jefferson's unifying vision for the grounds — the creation of an ornamental farm or *ferme ornée*. In a sketch of Monticello mountain around 1790, Jefferson planned for plots of experimental field crops to be juxtaposed with an adjacent planting of an elaborately conceived spiral labyrinth of scotch broom. In the text accompanying his sketch, Jefferson noted how he hoped to create a

1. West Front and
   Oval Flower Beds
2. Roundabout Walk and
   Flower Border
3. Weaver's Cottage, now used
   as offices
4. Levy Gravesite
5. Mulberry Row
6. Vegetable or Kitchen Garden
7. Garden Pavilion
8. Vineyard, Berry Squares,
   and Submural Beds
9. Orchard
10. First Roundabout
11. Grove

Illustration by Lucia C. Stanton

ferme ornée by "interspersing the articles of husbandry with the attributes of a garden." Jefferson was stamping the functional parts of his farm with his novel imagination by introducing ornamental conceits into his utilitarian landscape. In the same way, he planted flowering peach "fences" around his fields, and designed fish ponds which exploited function for ornamental purposes. The *ferme ornée* concept bridged the gap between the head and the heart, the agricultural scientist and the romantic designer.

South Piazza, or greenhouse, at Monticello

Greenhouse

Five large double-sashed windows in the Monticello greenhouse, or South Piazza, provided ample light and daylight warmth for tender plants. In 1811 Jefferson noted, "I have only a greenhouse, and have used that for only a very few articles. My frequent & long absences . . . render my efforts even for the few greenhouse plants I aim at, abortive." Although the greenhouse was strategically oriented toward the southeast and conveniently situated adjacent to Jefferson's cabinet and library, he noted growing only acacia (*Acacia farnesiana*, "the most delicious flowering shrub in the world"), sour orange, and lime trees from 1808, when the room was constructed, until 1811. A variety of tender southern African bulbs as well as Jerusalem cherry, oleander, gardenia, geranium, and cypress vine may also have been grown in the greenhouse, which possibly was also used as a propagation area for Jefferson's more precious horticultural specimens.

Poppy anemone (Anemone coronaria)

The Flower Gardens

The flowers come forth like the belles of the day, have their short reign of beauty and splendor, and retire, like them, to the more interesting office of reproducing their like. The Hyacinths and Tulips are off the stage, the Irises are giving place to the Belladonnas, as these will to the Tuberoses; as your mamma has done to you, my dear Anne, as you will do to the sisters of little John, and as I shall soon and cheerfully do to you all in wishing you a long, long, good night.

— Jefferson to Anne Cary Bankhead, 1811

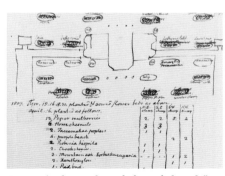

Jefferson's plan of the oval flower beds and "tree clumps," 1807 *(Courtesy of Historical Society of Pennsylvania)*

The flower gardens at Monticello not only functioned as a barometer to the passing seasons and as a stage upon which Jefferson related to his family, but they also served as an embellishment to a well conceived *ferme ornée*. Although there were earlier references to the flower "borders," it was not until 1807 that the flower gardens assumed their ultimate shape. Anticipating his retirement from the Presidency, Jefferson sketched a plan for twenty oval-shaped flower beds in the four corners or "angles" of the house. Each bed, an early nineteenth-century equivalent of our modern "island bed," was planted with a different flower, most of which had been forwarded as seeds or bulbs from Bernard McMahon.

West Lawn in late April with winding walk,
flower border, and fish pond

Oval Flower Beds

There were walks, and borders, and flowers, that I have never seen or heard of anywhere else. Some of them were in bloom from early in the spring until late in the winter.

— **Monticello Overseer, Edmund Bacon**

The range of flower species planted in 1807 reflected the scope of Jefferson's interests: Old World florists' flowers, local wildflowers, plants of curiosity, the fruits of botanical exploration. Some, such as the tulip, anemone, ranunculus, and hyacinth, were traditional bulblike plants commonly grown in improved forms as horticultural cultivars. Bulbs were especially popular in early American gardens because they could be shipped so easily. This partly explains why the tulip was the most commonly mentioned flower in the *Garden Book*. As well, McMahon had sent seeds of popular European garden flowers, such as the double form of "white" poppy (probably *Papaver rhoeas*), sweet William (*Dianthus barbatus*), carnation (*Dianthus caryophyllus*), pink (*Dianthus plumarius*), scarlet lychnis or Maltese cross (*Lychnis chalcedonica*), and everlasting pea (*Lathyrus latifolius*).

Two beds were planted with discoveries from the Lewis and Clark expedition: the "Columbian lilly" or *Fritillaria pudica*, and "Lewis' pea," perhaps Texas bluebonnet or *Lupinus subcarnosus*. Other native species included the *Jeffersonia*, or twinleaf, and the handsome, summer-blooming *Lobelia cardinalis*, or cardinal flower, which grows wild at the base of Monticello Mountain along the Rivanna River. Twenty-five percent of the flowers documented at Monticello are North American natives, and the gardens became, in part, a museum of New World botanical novelties. Finally, a few of the flowers planted in 1807 could be defined as curiosities, such as the winter cherry (*Physalis alkekengi*) with its lantern-like fruits and the blackberry lily (*Belamcanda chinensis*), named for its unusual berry-like seeds.

Jefferson's 1807 plan also included a planting of various shade and flower trees in the "angles" immediately adjacent to the house. He described the tree plantings as "clumps," and the scheme, surely inspired by his visit to English gardens twenty years earlier, was a continuation of similar plans in 1790, 1791, and 1804. Such an intensive planting, an effort to embower his house in shade, was an unusual concept at a time when many Virginia homes were surrounded by "swept yards" of raw, broom-swept earth.

Foxglove (Digitalis purpurea)

Roundabout Flower Border

I have an extensive flower border, in which I am fond of placing handsome *plants or* fragrant. *Those of mere curiosity I do not aim at, having too many other cares to bestow more than a moderate attention to them.*

— Jefferson to Bernard McMahon, 1811

In June of 1808 Jefferson sent his granddaughter, Anne, a plan for further plantings for the West Lawn: "I find that the limited number of our flower beds will too much restrain the variety of flowers in which we might wish to indulge, and therefore I have resumed an idea . . . of a winding walk . . . with a narrow border of flowers on each side. This would give abundant room for a great variety." The winding walk and the accompanying flower border were laid out in the spring of 1808, but by 1812, a need for a more systematic organization of the border required the division of the border into ten-foot sections, each compartment numbered and planted with a different flower.

The winding, relaxed lines of the walkway reflect Jefferson's interest in

Tulips along Roundabout walk in late April

"French mallow" (Malva sylvestris)

the latest, informal style of landscape design. The narrow flower border or ribbon beds, chopped into ten foot sections, would not be considered fashionable by modern standards, which celebrate the broad, mixed perennial border as the essence of garden art. The Roundabout walk and border is not a traditional "garden," which usually suggests a room outside, an enclosed retreat. Jefferson's flower beds and borders are exposed to the elements, open to the Piedmont Virginia landscape, intimately balanced with "the workhouse of nature."

A year-round planting plan for the flower gardens has not survived; however, Jefferson would occasionally note specific plantings in the oval or roundabout beds in his *Garden Book*. Many eighteenth-century discoveries were forwarded from the Jardin des Plantes in Paris, and nearly half the documented species planted at Monticello originated with McMahon. The flower gardens were not cared for by professional gardeners, but by Jefferson's daughters and granddaughters, often assisted by an elderly slave or by Jefferson himself, who would help with the design schemes, write labels, or set up a string line to assure straight rows.

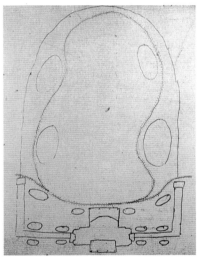

Jefferson's sketch of the Roundabout walk, from the back of a letter to his granddaughter, Anne Randolph, June 7, 1807. (From the Jefferson Papers, Courtesy of Massachusetts Historical Society)

The flower gardens virtually disappeared after Jefferson's death in 1826 but were restored by The Garden Club of Virginia between 1939 and 1941. Researchers found Jefferson's sketches of the beds and borders and deciphered the depression of the Roundabout flower walk by shining the headlights of their automobiles across the West Lawn at night. As well, perennial bulbs continued to flourish along the walk's border 115 years after Jefferson's death and so outlined its location.

Sweet William (Dianthus barbatus) *along the Roundabout flower border*

The Garden Today

Crown imperial lilies (Fritillaria imperialis)

Today, the gardens are planted as often as three times a year. In late April spring bulbs, especially tulips with their showy display of color, dominate the stage and unify the design and character of the gardens more than at any other time of year. By mid-May and continuing well into June, numerous biennials and perennials, from Sweet William to Canterbury Bells to Foxglove, come into bloom. They are complemented by the flowering of old rose species and hardy annuals, which thrive in the long, cool Virginia spring: sweet pea, larkspur, stock, poppy, and calendula.

By mid-July and continuing well into November, warm season annual flowers rule the garden. Featured are many of the species forms of what are today common flowers, including zinnia, geranium, heliotrope, French and African marigolds, snapdragons, and others. These species plants reflect the undeveloped flower that, in many cases, Jefferson would have cultivated. Generally, they have a low proportion of flowers to foliage, they are often leggier than modern cultivars, and some have simple, single flowers. The effect is one of a wildflower garden as the plants grow up and set seed, which is then collected and packaged for distribution.

In some cases, as with the florists' flowers Jefferson ordered from Bernard McMahon, ornamental species grown in the early nineteenth century were quite evolved — that is, the flowers were doubled, and their petals might be striped, fringed, or mottled. The restored gardens include some cultivars of columbine, sweet pea, primrose, clove pink, and wallflower that were known in the early 1800s. In other instances, when a flower grown by Jefferson was highly developed but is unavailable today, modern cultivars that resemble the earlier variety are grown. This is the case with hyacinths, tulips, anemones, and china asters.

Roses

Apothecary rose
(Rosa gallica officinalis)

Jefferson ordered thirty roses, including ten different species, from the William Prince Nursery of New York in 1791. These were planted "round the clumps of lilacs in front of the house," and should have evolved into an interesting shrubbery providing a succession of flowers through the spring. Jane Blair Smith, a friend of the Jefferson family, recalled that, "Under each low French window had been a flower bed, whose trellises were covered with yellow jessamine and climbing roses, a nest of sweets." Today, Jefferson's roses are distributed among several oval beds and on the East Front lawn, where the 1791 scheme has been recreated. Although they generally bloom only in late spring, older rose varieties are distinguished from their modern counterparts by a more graceful, shrub-like appearance.

Winding walk on West Lawn in early June. Flowers include lavender, sweet William, sweet peas, foxglove, corn poppies, larkspur, nicotiana, and Maltese cross.

Catalpa (Catalpa bignonioides) *and flowering dogwood* (Cornus florida) *on the edge of the West Lawn*

The Trees of Monticello

I never before knew the full value of trees. My house is entirely embosomed in
high plane-trees, with good grass below; and under them I breakfast, dine, write,
read, and receive my company. What would I not give that the trees planted
nearest round the house at Monticello were full grown —
— **Jefferson to Martha Randolph (from Philadelphia), 1793**

Jefferson undoubtedly ranked trees at the top of his hierarchical chart of
favorite garden plants. Visitors to Monticello were often given tours of the
grounds which included a rambling survey of what one guest described as
Jefferson's "pet trees." The image of lofty shade trees crowning the summit
was constantly reiterated by visitors to Monticello. Even in his most functional plantings, Jefferson exploited the ornamental qualities of 160 species
of trees. He planted groves of native and exotic trees; "clumps" of ornamentals adjacent to the house; *allees* of mulberry and honey locust along his road
network of Roundabouts; plantations of sugar maple and pecan; and living
peach tree fences to border his fields.

European larch (Larix decidua) *on the*
edge of the West Lawn dates from a
Jefferson-era planting around 1816.

While serving as Minister to France
between 1784 and 1789 Jefferson proudly distributed seeds of choice North American trees
to friends in Europe, continuing a tradition
begun with the earliest European explorers in
the New World. He has been described as "the
father of American forestry" for an 1804
planting of white pine and hemlock. His commitment to tree preservation was strongly suggested by a statement he allegedly made during
a dinner conversation at the President's House:
"I wish I was a despot that I might save the
noble, the beautiful trees that are daily falling
sacrifice to the cupidity of their owners, or the
necessity of the poor . . . . The unnecessary
felling of a tree, perhaps the growth of centuries, seems to me a crime little
short of murder." Thomas Jefferson's enthusiasm for the arboreal world was
unrelenting. Two months before his death, at the age of eighty-three, he
designed an arboretum for the University of Virginia. Such an epilogue to

View of West Front of Monticello with two "original" tulip poplars, or Liriodendron tulipifera, *(far right and left center)*

years of planting at Monticello was perhaps inspired by Jefferson's own adage: "Too old to plant trees for my own gratification I shall do it for posterity."

Native trees were commonly chosen for functional purposes. Jefferson planted an *allée* of the airy honey locust (*Gleditsia triacanthos*) along the first Roundabout at such a tight spacing, twenty-five feet, to suggest he desired the effect of an aerial hedge. He envisioned hedges and dark labyrinths composed of red cedar (*Juniperus virginiana*), which he also planted to encourage the local population of mockingbirds, his favorite bird. Jefferson chose the willow oak (*Quercus phellos*), described by a friend as "a favorite tree of his," to line Pennsylvania Avenue in the nation's capital (a scheme later abandoned) and, on one occasion, to encircle the west lawn at Monticello. He also intended rows of the slender and wispy black locust (*Robinia pseudoacacia*) to line either side of the lawn at the University of Virginia, where the species' sparse, delicate habit would not obscure the classical architectural motifs of the buildings he designed.

Many of the exotic trees Jefferson planted would fall in the "pet tree" category, regarded more as landscape specimens worthy of exaggerated care and attention than as sylvan workhorses. Some, like the golden-rain tree

Redbuds (Cercis canadensis) *and dogwoods on the edge of the Grove*

(*Koelreuteria paniculata*), were associated with close friends – in this case, Madame de Tessé of Paris. After a seed she had sent Jefferson in 1809 germinated in a flower pot, he wrote her, "I cherish [the seedling] with particular attentions, as it daily reminds me of the friendship with which you have honored me." The botanical exploitation of the orient, particularly of China and Japan, did not take place until well into the nineteenth century. The golden-rain tree, however, was among a number of oriental exceptions grown at Monticello; in fact, Jefferson may have been the first North American to grow this species.

Several specimens, original trees, have survived the inhospitable environment of mountaintop existence. These include a red cedar (*Juniperus virginiana*), a species which, surprisingly, Jefferson said was introduced into Albemarle County; a sugar maple (*Acer saccharum*), the lone survivor of his efforts to create sugar plantations in central Virginia; a European larch (*Larix decidua*), a deciduous conifer on the edge of the West Lawn; and two impressive tulip poplars (*Liriodendron tulipifera*) adjacent to the house. A purple or copper beech (*Fagus sylvatica 'atropunicea'*), now growing in "an angle" of the west side of the house, is a replacement for a Jefferson era tree blown down in the 1950s.

The Grove

Within a few days I shall bury myself in the groves of Monticello and become a mere spectator to passing events.
— **Jefferson to Alexander von Humboldt, 1809**

Umbrella magnolia (Magnolia tripetala)

In 1806 Jefferson drew a sketch of Monticello mountain and designated eighteen acres on the northwestern side as the "grove." He envisioned a pleasure ground where "the canvas at large must be Grove, of the largest trees trimmed very high, so as to give it the appearance of open ground." Jefferson intended the Grove to be an ornamental forest with the undergrowth removed, the trees pruned and thinned, and the woodland "broken by clumps of thicket, as the open grounds of the English are broken by clumps of trees."

The Grove also included a planting of ornamental trees in an open area adjacent to the West Lawn. They were chosen for the contrasting textures of their foliage and included wild crab (*Malus coronaria*), chinaberry (*Melia azedarach*), umbrella magnolia (*Magnolia tripetala*), aspen (*Populus tremuloides*), and catalpa (*Catalpa bignonioides*). Some of these species are not hardy or adaptable to a mountaintop in central Virginia. Substitutions were inevitably made, and the upper part of the Grove probably became an arboretum of Mr. Jefferson's "pet trees."

In many ways, the lower or woodland part of the Grove represented Jefferson's ideal American landscape, where "gardens may be made without expense. We have only to cut out the superabundant plants." He said that "under the constant, beaming, almost vertical sun of Virginia, shade is our Elysium." The mature, deciduous forest should be further refined with the introduction of vistas, glades, hardy perennial flowers, and a ground cover of turf. He also sketched a plan for thickets of shrubs arranged in a spiral pattern to suggest an informal labyrinth. Furthermore, Jefferson hoped "to procure a Buck-elk, to be as it were, monarch of the wood," and suggested stumps should be left "where they might be picturesque."

Although it is uncertain how much of the Grove was actively main-

The lower or wooded section of the Grove, where "gardens may be made without expense. We have only to cut out the superabundant plants."

tained by Jefferson, a project was begun to recreate the concept in 1977. The existing forest was cleared and thinned, young trees, shrubs, and herbaceous flowers planted, and vistas, glades, and thickets introduced as Jefferson had envisioned.

The Vegetable or Kitchen Garden at Monticello

Red cabbage (Brassica oleracea) *and maple leaf* (Acer rubrum)

The Vegetable Garden

"I have lived temperately, eating little animal food, and that . . . as a condiment for the vegetables, which constitute my principal diet."
— **Jefferson to Vine Utley, 1819**

When Jefferson referred to his "garden," he, like most early Americans, was reserving the term for his vegetable garden, a 1,000-foot-long terrace on the southeastern side of his "little mountain." Although the garden served as a food source for the family table, it also functioned as a kind of laboratory where he experimented with seventy different species of vegetables. While Jefferson would grow as many as forty types of bean and seventeen lettuce varieties, his use of the scientific method selectively eliminated inferior sorts: "I am curious to select one or two of the best species or variety of every garden vegetable, and to reject all others from the garden to avoid the dangers of mixing or degeneracy."

The garden evolved over many years, beginning in 1770 when crops were grown along the contours of the slope. Terracing was introduced in 1806, and by 1812, gardening activity was at its peak. The terrace or garden plateau, literally hewed from the side of the mountain, was described as a "hanging garden" by one visitor. The garden's dramatic setting is enhanced by the pavilion, perched atop the massive garden wall at the half-way point of the terrace. Distinguished by its double sash windows, Chinese railing, and pyramidal roof, the pavilion was used by Jefferson as a quiet retreat where he could read in the evening. It was reputedly blown down in a violent wind storm in the 1820s but was reconstructed in 1984 based on Jefferson's notes and archaeological excavations.

The Garden Pavilion was reconstructed in 1984 based on Jefferson's notes and archealogical excavations of its foundation.

The main part of the two-acre garden is divided into twenty-four "squares," or growing plots, and, at least in 1812, the squares were arranged according to which part of the plant was being harvested — whether "fruits" (tomatoes, beans), "roots" (beets), or "leaves" (lettuce, cabbage). Jefferson used the Northwest Border to plant tomatoes, cucumbers, and peas very early in the season. Because of the warmth radiated by the grassy bank, this border should have provided him with a decided advantage in the annual spring pea contests. At the base of the wall, below the garden, Jefferson successfully grew figs in "Submural beds," which were also situated to create a uniquely warm setting. The site and situation of the garden enabled Jefferson to extend the growing season into the winter months and provided an amenable microclimate for tender vegetables such as the French artichoke. Because of favorable air drainage on a small mountaintop, late spring frosts are rare, and the first freezing temperatures in the fall rarely occur before Thanksgiving.

Aside from the garden pavilion, Jefferson occasionally considered other ornamental features for the terrace. He discussed planting different flowering shades of "arbor" bean ("purple, red, scarlet, and white"), arranged adjacent rows of purple, white, and green sprouting broccoli, or even white and purple eggplant, and he bordered his tomato square with sesame or okra, a rather unusual juxtaposition of plant textures. Cherry trees were also planted along the "long, grass walk" at the edge of the garden above the wall.

Salads were an important part of Jefferson's diet. He would note the planting of lettuce and radishes every two weeks through the growing season, grow interesting greens like orach, corn salad, endive, and nasturtium, and plant sesame in order to manufacture a suitable salad oil. While the English pea is considered his favorite vegetable, he also cherished figs, asparagus, artichokes, and such "new" vegetables as tomatoes, eggplant, broccoli, and cauliflower. While Jefferson cultivated common crops like cucumbers, cabbages, and beans (both "snaps" for fresh use and "haricots" that were dried), he also prized his sea kale (*Crambe maritima*), a perennial cabbage-like species whose spring sprouts were blanched in pots, then cut and prepared like asparagus.

The cultural directions in Bernard McMahon's *Calendar* — for manuring the garden, interplanting lettuce and radishes, and planting cucumbers in hogsheads — were followed diligently in the Monticello garden. McMahon also sent Jefferson important vegetable varieties such as Leadman's Dwarf pea, Egyptian onion, Early York and Sugarloaf cabbage, red celery, and red globe artichoke. Much of the vegetable gardening itself seemed to have been

delegated to the more elderly slaves, who were sometimes referred to as the "veteran aids." Jefferson's daughter, Martha, in 1792, said the garden "does not bear close examination, the weeds having taken possession of much the greater part of it. Old George is so slow that by the time he has got to the end of his labour he has it all to do over again." However, Jefferson's meticulous notes on the day when peas were sowed or beans harvested suggests he was on site, perhaps directing the work. Years after Jefferson's death, one of his slaves, Isaac, recalled, "For amusement he would work sometimes in

Tennis-ball lettuce (Lactuca sativa)

The leaves, seeds, and flowers of the nasturtium (Tropaeolum majus) *were used by Jefferson in salads.*

the garden for half an hour at a time in right good earnest in the cool of the evening."

The recreation of the Monticello vegetable garden began in 1979 with two years of archaeological excavations that attempted to confirm details of the documentary evidence. Archaeologists uncovered the remnants of the stone wall, exposed the foundation of the garden pavilion, and discovered evidence of the location of the entrance gate, which then ensured the squares were laid out according to Jefferson's specifications. While harvested vegetables are today distributed to Monticello employees, the garden also serves as a preservation seed bank of Jefferson and nineteenth-century vegetable varieties. These are often allowed to set seed, which is then collected and either saved or distributed.

Jefferson often listed vegetable varieties according to the person from whom he received the seed ("Leitch's pea"), its place of origin ("Tuscan bean"), a physical characteristic such as color ("yellow carrot"), or season of harvest ("Forward pea"). "Leitch's pea" is not only unavailable from commercial sources today, but there is no description of its qualities in the garden literature of the last two centuries. The collection of Jefferson's 250 vegetable varieties is a complex challenge. In many cases, the varieties in the garden were known in the nineteenth century and serve as substitutes for the originals grown by Jefferson.

Vegetables featured in the garden include three English pea varieties: Prince Albert, introduced around 1840 and apparently identical to the Early Frame grown by Jefferson; Blue Prussian, the parent of Alaska, which was named for a nineteenth-century trans-Atlantic steamer that crossed the ocean in forty-five days; and Champion of England, the oldest wrinkled seed variety still in cultivation. Other notable varieties include Tennis-ball lettuce, the predecessor to the Boston types and Jefferson's second favorite lettuce variety; Arikara bean, which had been collected by the Lewis and Clark expedition from Dakota Indian tribes and was perhaps first grown in eastern North America at Monticello; and White Pine strawberry, an excellent representative of the earliest breeding efforts that resulted in our modern straw-

Arbor in garden covered with hyacinth bean (Dolichos lablab) *in late summer*

berry. Hyacinth beans (*Dolichos lablab*) blanket a recreated arbor to duplicate Jefferson's proposed decorative planting of "arbor" beans along the "long walk of the garden." Their lush, deep-purple leaves, smooth, burgundy seed pods, and showy lavender flowers provide an unforgettable visual feast.

Green Gage plum
from William Hooker's
Pomona Londinensis, *1818*

Jefferson's Fruit Garden with Green Gage plums, the northeast Vineyard, garden wall, and pavilion

Seckel Pear

Fruit Garden

When he [Jefferson] walked in the garden and would call the children to go with him, we raced after and before him, and we were made perfectly happy by this permission to accompany him. Not one of us in our wildest moods ever placed a foot on one of the garden beds, for that would violate one of his rules. He would gather fruit for us, seek out the ripest figs, or bring down the cherries from on high above our heads with a long stick, at the end of which there was a hook and a little net bag.

— Virginia Jefferson Trist, 1839

Monticello's Fruit Garden, or "Fruitery" as Jefferson called it in 1814, sprawled below the vegetable garden and included the 400-tree South Orchard; two small vineyards ("Northeast" and "Southwest"); berry squares of currants, gooseberries, and raspberries; a nursery where Jefferson propagated fruit trees and special garden plants; and "submural beds," where figs and strawberries were grown to take advantage of the warming microclimate created by the stone wall. On the other side of the mountain, Jefferson's North Orchard was reserved for cider apples and seedling peaches (peach trees grown from seed).

Ripening Brunswick figs (Ficus carica)

Both the Monticello Fruitery (including the South Orchard) and the North Orchard reflected the two distinct forms of fruit growing that emerged in eighteenth-century Virginia. The North Orchard was typical of the "Field" or "Farm" orchards found on most middle-class farms: it was large, on average 200 trees, and consisted of only apple or peach trees. The fruit was harvested for cider, brandy, or as livestock feed. There is some truth to one historian's tongue-in-cheek remark that it was a significant event when Americans began eating their fruit rather than drinking it. The trees in these utilitarian orchards were usually propagated from seed, resulting in unpredictable variations and few named varieties, and the orchard received little horticultural attention such as pruning or pest control.

On the other hand, the Monticello Fruitery resembled a gentleman's Fruit Garden in the Old World horticultural tradition, and was similar to the diverse recreational plantings of other wealthy Virginians such as George Washington. The trees, often planted with small fruits and even ornamentals, were grafted and included a wide spectrum of European varieties and unusual species like apricots and almonds, reserved, according to Jefferson, for the "precious refreshment" of their fancy fruit. The Fruitery at Monticello, however, was unique because it was both an Old World Fruit Garden and colonial Virginia "Farm Orchard." Seedling peaches and Virginia cider apples were planted alongside French apricots and Spanish almonds. Its sprawling American scale was defined by manageable units: an intensively cultivated nursery, terraced vineyards, berry squares of small fruit, fig gardens, blocks of cherry trees, and plots of precious, experimental field crops planted between the orchard rows. Like Jefferson himself, it represented the best of the European heritage combined with a distinctive New World vitality and personality.

Blossoming peach trees (Prunus persica) *in the South Orchard*

The Site

It was a fine garden. There were vegetables of all kinds, grapes, figs, and the finest variety of fruit. I have never seen such a place for fruit. It was so high that it never failed.

— Monticello Overseer, Edmund Bacon

Although not elevated enough for general climatic changes, Monticello is high enough (867 feet) that, during the spring and fall months as cold air settles in the bottomlands, the warmer air rises over the mountain — effectively preventing frost damage to blooming fruit trees. The Fruitery's southeastern exposure was a crucial factor in determining which species could be successfully grown. Tender trees — almonds and pomegranates — and fruits friendly to a warm, sunny environment like peaches and grapes were ideal for such a setting. Nevertheless, pears, apples, European plums, gooseberries, and currants suffered from the artificially southern climate. This partly explains why the sun-loving peach was Jefferson's favorite fruit tree and why he was only successful in growing apple varieties acclimated to the South.

Propagation

In theory, every time one plants a seed of an apple or peach, the ensuing seedling is a new variety. The only way of duplicating the parent is by asexual means – budding or grafting. Most Virginia "Farm Orchards" were planted with seedling trees, partly because it was simpler, partly because any fruit would suffice when apples were harvested for cider or peaches for brandy. The planting of seedling orchards was a significant development in the definition of American horticulture because the seedling trees would sometimes produce exceptional fruit, a tasty apple or a hardy peach, which would then be named and preserved by budding and grafting. For the first time, unique New World cultivars marked the dawn of North American plant breeding.

Although Jefferson believed most stone fruits (peaches, plums, etc.) could be propagated from seed and that seedling trees were healthier, he usually grafted or budded the trees he planted in the South Orchard in order to preserve the dessert qualities of a Newtown Pippin apple or Carnation cherry. Outside specialists, or his Scottish gardener Robert Bailey, were often contracted to graft apples and pears or "innoculate" (or bud) cherries.

Nurseries

Jefferson had at least two nurseries: the "old nursery" below the garden wall and the terraced "new nursery," which was an extension of the northeast end of the vegetable garden. Here he propagated seeds and cuttings he received from friends and neighbors. Jefferson occasionally purchased plants from commercial sources, such as the William Prince nursery on Long Island, considered the nation's first, yet his home nurseries provided most of the plants for the Fruitery. The list of plants he grew in them included his favorite species; he propagated thirteen kinds of shrubs, forty-one species of ornamental trees, twenty-six vegetable varieties, six kinds of grasses, eleven nut trees, and fifty-three fruit tree varieties in his nurseries. They were the heart of his pomological, if not horticultural, world.

Fences

The Fruitery (as well as the vegetable garden) was enclosed with a variety of materials during Jefferson's fruit growing career: board fences, living hawthorn hedges, and even ditches that functioned as cattle guards. The most ambitious enclosure was the paling fence. Ten feet high, the fence extended nearly three quarters of a mile around the entire complex. The palings, or thin boards, were "so near as not to let even a young hare in." Although the paling gates were secured with a lock and key, overseer Edmund Bacon recalled fruit fights that arose when a band of schoolboys, rivals to Jefferson's grandson, Thomas Jefferson Randolph, broke down the palings and "did a great deal of damage" while pelting each other with unripe apples and peaches. Although most nineteenth-century orchards were fenced, it was customary for travellers through the Virginia countryside to help themselves to bearing fruit. Wayside orchards were considered part of the common domain.

The South Orchard

Between 1769 and 1814 Jefferson planted as many as 1,031 fruit trees in his South Orchard. It was organized into a grid pattern in which he set out approximately eighteen varieties of apple, thirty-eight of peach, fourteen cherry, twelve pear, twenty-three plum, three nectarine, eight almond, eight apricot, and one quince. The earliest plantings, before 1780, reflect the experimental orchard of a young man eager to import Mediterranean culture to Virgina and included olives, almonds, pomegranates, and figs. However, the mature plantings after 1810 included mostly species and varieties that thrived through the hot, humid summers and cold, rainy winters of central Virginia, such as seedling peaches or Virginia cider apples, or Jefferson's favorite fancy fruits like the Esopus Spitzenburg apple. Many of Jefferson's trials with European fruit varieties were unsuccessful. For example, while he planted twenty-three plum varieties during his gardening career at Monticello, by 1811 the orchard contained only two plum trees. The restoration of the South Orchard began in 1981 and was an attempt to recreate his mature, 1811 plan.

Monticello's Fruit Garden extends below the garden wall, and includes the South Orchard, two vineyards, and the nursery (below). The white-blossoming tree is the flowering dogwood.

Royal George peaches harvested from the South Orchard

The Luxury of the Peach

Breast of Venus peach from Giorgio Gallesio's Pomona Italiana, *1817*

Jefferson planted as many as thirty-eight varieties of peach at a time when there were few cultivars available. In 1811 the South Orchard included 160 peach trees, far more than any other species. When Jefferson wrote his granddaughter in 1815 that "we abound in the luxury of peach," he was repeating a theme expressed by colonial fruit growers and even the first natural historians of the New World. Although the peach tree is an oriental native, it was introduced into Florida in the sixteenth century and brought north by Indians. Seedlings escaped from orchards so readily that many early botanists were awed by the abundance of "wild" peaches throughout the Southeast. The peach was one of the first North American weeds. Peach orchards also thrived, partly because introduced insects and disease had not spread enough to be a problem. Peaches were so prolific they were commonly fed to the hogs.

Peaches were also popular because they were easy to grow, trees bore fruit soon after planting, and they could be propagated simply from seed. Jefferson dried the fruit and also made mobby, a peach beverage common in Virginia. He planted thousands of peach trees along his fields as ornamental fences and also envisioned this fast-growing tree as a forestry product to provide wood for his fireplaces. But Jefferson also tried to assemble a collection of peach varieties for the table: Heath Cling, Oldmixon Cling, Morris' Red Rareripe — the first American peach varieties, and Italian varieties previously unknown in the country — the Alberges, Vaga Loggia, and Apple.

The Democratic Apple

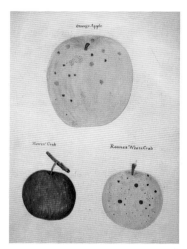

Some early American apple varieties, including Hewes' Crab, from Coxe's unpublished "A View Toward the Cultivation of Fruit Trees"

Just as the peach represented the luxurious fertility of the New World, the apple came to symbolize the diversity of America's melting pot culture. One modern source listed the names of nearly 17,000 apple varieties that appeared in nineteenth-century American periodicals. Hundreds of varieties were available to Virginia gardeners around 1800, many of them cider apples, most well-adapted to the severe continental climate. Jefferson, however, concentrated on only four cultivars either unequalled for cider production or unsurpassed as dessert fruits.

The Hewes' Crab was the most important horticultural cultivar in eighteenth-century Virginia. This small, maverick apple appears to be a cross between the apple of pomology and the native crabapple (*Malus angustifolia*), and it thrived in Virginia when more northern or European apples failed. Crushing the juicy Hewes' Crab for cider was like "squeezing a wet sponge." The Taliaferro was Jefferson's favorite: "the best cyder apple existing . . . nearer to the silky Champagne than any other." Unfortunately, it has disappeared from cultivation and remains Monticello's mystery apple. When comparing the fruits of Europe and America, Jefferson wrote from Paris, "They have no apple to compare with our Newtown Pippin." Known later as the Albemarle Pippin, this apple supported a large industry in Jefferson's home county based on export abroad. Like the Pippin, the Spitzenburg originated in New York and ruled the nineteenth-century pomological charts when apples were often critically reviewed and competitively rated.

Figs growing in the "submural beds" at the base of the garden wall below the bean arbor
Below, Seckle pear, from Coxe's "A View Toward the Cultivation of Fruit Trees"

Other Fruit Trees

Jefferson's enthusiasm for his experimental trials was reflected by his proclamations on superior varieties. The Carnation was his favorite cherry, "so superior to all others that no other deserves the name of cherry." The Seckel pear, which originated near Philadelphia, was "the finest pear I've tasted since I left France & equalled the best pear there." The Peach apricot, which he introduced from France, was "the finest fruit which grows in Europe," and the Marseilles fig was "the finest fig I've ever seen." Indeed, Jefferson's 130 varieties of fruit trees represented the finest cultivars available to an early nineteenth-century gardener.

Sangiovese grape in the Northeast Vineyard

Vineyards

I expect to be gratified with the great desideratum of making at home a good wine.
— **Jefferson to Levin Gale, 1816**

Thomas Jefferson has been described as America's "first distinguished viticulturist" and "the greatest patron of wine and winegrowing that this country has yet had." Although he aspired to make a Monticello-grown wine, his continual replanting of the vineyards suggests a perennial and losing battle with grape cultivation. But Jefferson was not alone. The successful cultivation in eastern North America of *Vitis vinifera*, the classic European wine species, was virtually impossible until the development of modern pesticides controlled such destructive pests as black rot and phylloxera, an aphid-like root louse. Many native grapes were more effectively grown, yet the poor quality of the resultant wine impeded progress in the development of an established industry. The history of grape culture at Monticello suggests Jefferson's unrelenting oscillation between a desire to grow the difficult yet rewarding *vinifera*, and the possibilities of well-adapted New World alternatives – the fox grape (*Vitis labrusca*) and the Scuppernong variety of the southern muscadine (*V. rotundifolia*).

The two vineyards, Northeast (9,000 square feet) and Southwest (16,000 square feet), were ideally sited for grape growing in the heart of the South Orchard below the garden wall. The 1807 planting of 287 rooted vines and cuttings of twenty-four European grape varieties was the most ambitious of seven experiments. The vineyards were organized into seventeen narrow terraces, each reserved for specific varieties Jefferson had received from three sources, two of which were in Italy. Many of these

Muscat Blanc grape

vinifera cultivars had probably never been grown in the New World. Such a varietal rainbow, many of them table grapes, represents the vineyard of a plant collector, an experimenter rather than a serious wine maker. When this scheme failed, probably because the vines were dead on arrival or were not planted properly, Jefferson became more committed to the alternative possibilities of native American vines.

Jefferson's 1807 plan for the Northeast vineyard was restored in 1985, and the Southwest vineyard was replanted in 1992. Jefferson's European varieties were grafted onto the more resilient native rootstock to encourage hardiness and pest resistance. Because of a documentery suggestion that vines were "espaliered," a permanent structure based on an eighteenth-century American grape treatise was constructed. Three hundred bottles of a blended white wine were made from the harvest of 1988 and the restored vineyards continue to serve as an experimental garden of unusual varieties grown without toxic pesticides.

Northeast Vineyard, Garden Wall, and Pavilion

Dianthus 'Painted Lady'

The Thomas Jefferson Center
for Historic Plants

The species form of heliotrope (Heliotropium arborescens), of which Jefferson said, "a delicious flower; the smell rewards the care," and the foliage of swamp sunflower (Helianthus angustifolia)

The culmination of the restoration of Jefferson's gardens at Monticello was the opening of the Center for Historic Plants in 1987 — an educational garden center devoted to the collection, preservation, and distribution of plants known in early American gardens. The program focuses on Thomas Jefferson's horticultural interests, but also covers the history of plants cultivated in America up to 1900, as well as native plants, a group of special interest to Jefferson himself. Herbaceous ornamentals are a specialty of the Center, fulfilling a unique need in the movement to preserve the germplasm of the past.

The Garden Shop, open from late March into November, is located at the Monticello Shuttle Station. Historic plants, heirloom seeds, and books on the history of garden plants are available at the Shop. *Twinleaf*, the annual newsletter and seed list of the Center, also features fifty species of Monticello and CHP seeds and a choice selection of books on garden history for mail order purchase. For *Twinleaf*, write: The Thomas Jefferson Center for Historic Plants, Monticello, P. O. Box 316, Charlottesville, Virginia, 22902.